A Risk Worth Taking

Written by DAVID AUGSBURGER
Photos by PAUL M. SCHROCK

MOODY PRESS
CHICAGO

contents

A Personal Note

I lived my younger years trying to achieve my identity by high performance, to demonstrate my ability by clever speech, and to show my brilliance by deep questions.

Slowly, I came to realize that the most questionable things about me were my pretensions to sufficiency, my fantasies of achieving perfection by denying and ignoring my own inadequacies.

Slowly, I became aware that the ability needed was usability in service to God.

The responsibility He asks is ability to respond to Christ!

Which Way Joy?

Happy are the strong, for they are always on top.

Happy are the rich, for theirs is the right to live in luxury.

Happy are the ruthless, for they get their own way.

Happy are the well-armed, for they trust in self-defense.

Happy are the proud, for they are content with themselves.

Happy are the clever, for theirs is success.

Happy are the well-adjusted, for they feel no guilt.

Happy are the selfish, for they look out for themselves.

Happy are the apathetic, for they are the comfortable.

A rather uncommon set of beatitudes? No, an all too common series of attitudes.

Jesus Christ insisted that happiness lies in the other direction. Happiness is found in life for others!

Free to Fail

God has not asked us to be successful. He has asked us to be faithful.

He does not hold us responsible for success. He holds us responsible for obedience.

He does not demand that we accomplish great things, but that we accept the small.

It's not the success that matters. It's faithfulness. To Jesus Christ.

Knowing that God accepts us in spite of our failures, we don't need to hide them, or even fear them. In following Christ, we're free to fail. He never promised us that we would always be safe, be right, be successful.

He only promised us freedom, meaning, and joy. Forever. Our part? Faithfulness.

Not success. Faithfulness.

A Risk Worth Taking

Life is risk. The risk of failure and despair.

Love is risk. The risk of rejection and suffering.

Faith is risk. The risk of commitment and sacrifice.

You bet your life on something or other, or you do not live. What's your bet?

I bet my life on God—the God shown us in Jesus Christ. I wager that life is lived at its fullest and best when lived in the style of life shown us in Jesus Christ.

If God does not exist, I lose nothing and I still win the benefits of a rewarding, richly relational Christian life.

But if God does exist, then I win all. My best bet then is to bet that God IS. My chances to win are two to one.

Strange As It Seems

We surrender to win.
We receive to give.
We give away to keep.
We suffer to get well.
We are strong when weak.
We accept limitation to experience freedom.
We die to live.

Self-Improvement
Is Not Enough

One of the fond ideas many of us have is that it is possible for us to improve ourselves by our own efforts.

Jesus didn't accept this. He insisted that, if a man is going to change, he must *be* changed; that, if a man is going to improve, he must be transformed from within.

Here's how. Confess that you have been a sinner. Turn your back on all that you know to have been wrong. Tell the Lord Jesus you do not want to make just a few improvements, but you want the change to be complete.

Turn toward Him in glad obedience and say, "I pledge to be Yours. Enter my life and change me completely. Let me follow You from this day forward in life."

And then ask for the gift of His presence, the Holy Spirit, to be within you.

You can be a new person. Not a patched-up old person, but a man made new in Jesus Christ.

As We Were

God loved us as we were—
   When we were enemies,
hostile, angry, in revolt,
   God loved.
   When we were alone,
proud, withdrawn, in solitude,
   God loved.
   When we were bent,
turned-in in evil, in sin,
   God loved.
He came in Jesus to say, "I love you—"
   Not because of what we were,
   not because of what we might be,
   not because of what we would become.
      He simply loved us.
      He cared.
      He gave us grace
      (undeserved love)
      in Jesus.
   God loved us as we were.

Faith in a Person

One day, in the midst of my doubting, one of the greatest thoughts I've ever thought was suggested to me by a friend. If God is—if God lives—if God loves—then you don't approach Him as if He were a thing, an idea, a philosophy. You approach Him as a Person. With trust. With love.

Faith is like responding to friendship, not adopting a philosophy.

You believe men. You take their word for a lot of things. Not blindly. But you accept it until matters are proven otherwise.

Now if you can extend credit—or credibility—to a man, how dare you refuse it to God?

Venture. Explore. Experiment. And then experience.

A Man for All Men

Jesus was a man for all men, a Christ for all cultures. His language was Hebrew but His thoughts were universal.

He spoke truth any man can feel, told stories in which every man sees himself, pictured life as every man longs to live it, and communicated the loving acceptance for which all men hunger.

He is a man for all men—a human Jesus who hurts where we hurt, laughs where we laugh, feels with the best of our feelings, and points us toward what men of all cultures should be.

And a divine Christ who grips our lives with strength where we are powerless to become what we should be. And then transforms us—thought by thought, emotion after emotion—into His own image and likeness.

Venture into Light

Every man has a cave of his own. A cavern of retreat. A place of safe withdrawal.

At times he ventures into the light. But then the threat of new truth breaks upon him and he retreats. Back to the warm darkness of his cave. Back to safety.

But truth once seen is hard to forget. Truth tugs. It draws. Like light. It grows on him. And when at last it is irresistible and he stumbles from his seclusion to stand blinking in the painful clarity of fresh insight, he will see things about himself, his life, and his destiny that he has never known before.

And the nearer he gets to truth, the more it looks like the face of Christ.

Jesus Is No Additive

Weekends boring? Try an additive (in box, capsule, carton, or bottles).

Marriage going stale? Car getting sluggish? Work becoming tedious? Food tasting flat? Energy lagging? Get an additive!

STP your car; Geritol your glands; enzyme your wash—choose your additive.

Values running low? Meaning draining out of your life? Perhaps a shot of religion might help. Give God a try. He's the greatest additive of all. (Tongue-in-cheek, of course.)

Jesus is no additive. He offers no additives.

Jesus is an alternative. He is not an optional accessory for the well-appointed man.

Jesus is an alternative to all that we are. He is a contrast to all that we habitually choose to be and do.

And He offers us the freedom to take a new way in life. Not an additive to our old way, but an alternative way of life.

Live a Little Recklessly

If you stop giving the moment it begins to hurt, you never discover true generosity.

If you stop serving the moment it pinches you, you never discover sacrifice and its rewards.

If you quit loving the moment it becomes difficult, you never discover compassion.

If you refuse to forgive in the moment that cries for revenge, you never discover the grace of unconditional forgiveness.

If you hesitate to share yourself the moment it costs, you never discover intimate fellowship.

Joy comes to those who don't know when to quit, who can't draw a line, who live, give, and forgive a little recklessly.

**Live your faith.
Light the world.**

Forgiveness Is...

. . . acceptance given another when both of you know that what he did is unacceptable.

. . . forgetfulness toward the old justifications for keeping an insult or injury alive.

. . . awareness that the forgiver also has constant need of forgiveness.

. . . reconciliation that receives the other person without the assurance of complete restitution and making of amends.

. . . recognition that forgiver and forgiven are equals, each needing the other, each incomplete without the other.

And so, before God, each drops all charges, refuses all self-justifications, and forgives. And forgives. "Seventy times seven," as Jesus said.

No Use for People

People are people. Not pawns, playthings, or poker chips.

People are persons. They are not usable. Collectable. Tradeable. Discardable. Forgettable.

People are perishable. People are priceless. People are irreplaceable. People are to be respected responsibly.

When I discover I'm being manipulated for someone else's advantage, when I sense that I'm being used to build another's ego, to bolster another's pride, to advance another's personal power or prestige, I don't like it. Do you?

God made things to be used, and people to be loved.

Under the Influence
of Affluence

Money. 200 proof. Taken straight or mixed with many lovely things, it's the most intoxicating substance known to man.

Like any intoxication, the first flush of wealth may bring an illusion of exhilaration, of accelerated pleasures. It may inebriate a man with the gentle blush of success, giving him a false sense of well-being. As he gradually slips under the influence, the comfort and safety of wealth deadens insight and depresses his perspective on reality.

Affluence is the perfect anesthesia for helping a man forget the pain of others. It anesthetizes conscience, compassion, and common concern. At last it isolates a person, cutting him off from both God and man.

He's under the influence. The influence of affluence.

To one affluence addict Jesus said, "Kick the habit, cold turkey; then come and follow Me."

But he went away sad, for he was hooked.

None Are So Blind
As Those Who Will Not See

Apathy is the lowest point of human morality. To say, "I couldn't care less," is to deny all human values and virtues.

Indifference is the basest response of human emotion. To see the needs of fellow beings and feel no concern or compassion is a living death.

The ultimate sinner is not the pimp or the prostitute, not the thief or embezzler, not the rapist or murderer. The chief of sinners is he who knows the truth, senses the right, feels the morally responsible way, and closes his eyes.

This is unpardonably deliberate blindness.

"That's the tragedy of it," Jesus once said. "Men walk blindly by the light, eyes closed tight, because they refuse to see."

"You calling us blind?" some asked.

"You asked the question. You must know the answer," He replied.

A Barefoot Bluff?

To believe one thing and do another is to be a barefoot bluff.

Faith is shoes—for wearing, for walking, for working—all week.

Faith is not some static, nebulous nothing a man slips into on Sunday.

Faith is not something you say at the right time and place. Faith is something you are. Everywhere. All the time.

What a man believes should soon become what a man is—if there's any integrity about him.

Back up your claim to know Christ truly, by following Him daily in life.

BOOKS
MAGAZINES
Complete
Nudity
NOT OBSCENE
U.S. SUPREME
COURT RULING
NO ONE
UNDER 18
ADMITTED

Develop Inner Immunity

Isolate a child from all possibilities of infection, and he grows up susceptible to all.

Separate a young man from all contact with evil; and when he is suddenly faced with the opportunity, he has little power to refuse it.

It is not the sterile safety of perfectly pure surroundings that we need, but inner resistance. Inner immunity to evil.

Inner immunity is not achieved through isolation from sin and sinners. Inner immunity is developed through contact, conflict, and conquest of evil.

Immaturity needs the assistance of a few fences. But as a person demonstrates his ability to say no to what is unquestionably evil or even what is questionably suspect, then the guardrails become less and less important. Christlike living becomes so captivating that fences become unnecessary.

Time Is People

Cash in your minutes, bankroll your days, turn your life into gold. That's the good word if time is money.

But for a man whose values are straight, time is people. He puts persons ahead of things.

Listening to people is not a waste of time. Listening to them is loving them. Talking with people is giving a gift of concern and acceptance. Helping people is the best possible use of time.

Jesus invested His time in people. He gave them His time to listen, to help, to hurt with their hurts.

Time is life as a person among persons. As Jesus lived it. Supremely.

"Double-Speak" Spoken Here

"I love humanity; it's people I can't stand."

"I'm in favor of open housing, just not in my neighborhood."

"I'm against pollution, but my business can't afford to change just now."

"I like all people; it's just the crew I have to work with that I can't take."

Can you speak "double-speak"? It says, "I agree in principle, but it's out of the question for me in practice."

Sin is choosing the generality to avoid the uncomfortable specific. It's preferring the abstract to the concrete.

Sin is stopping with good intentions when the real point is caring enough to act—to love— in the Jesus way.

The Jesus way is the I-love-you-enough-to-help-now way.

42

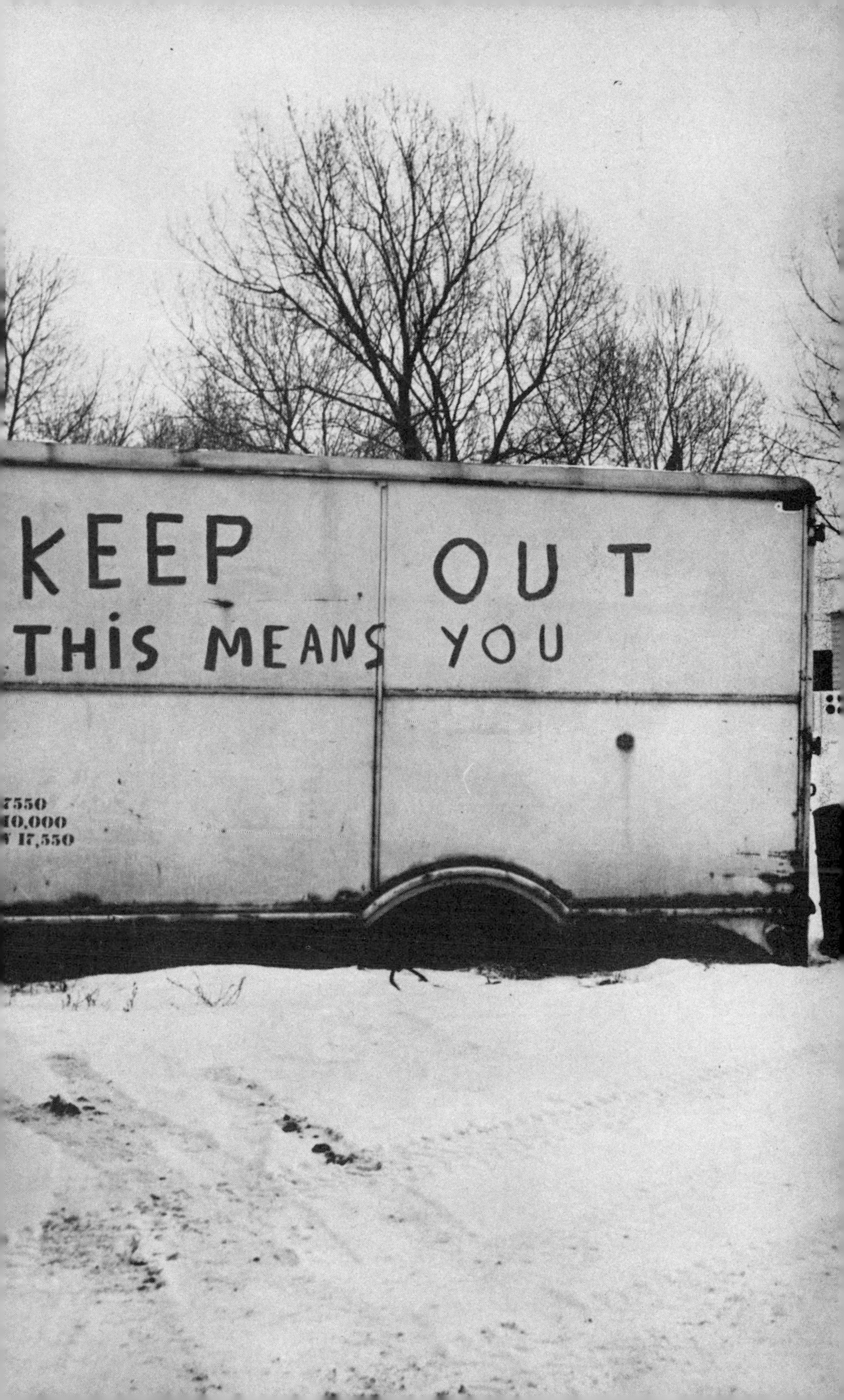
KEEP OUT
THIS MEANS YOU

More Than Words

It's a sobering discovery to realize—to comprehend—that people will be little changed, little moved, little affected by what you say. But look out for what you are!

That's how it is in communication. YOU are being heard, not your words.

You cannot NOT communicate. You are the communication.

Your words about love are believed when they are seen in act, not when stated as fact.

Your love is received when it is felt, not when it is said in syllables.

Why not just be the love of Christ to others. Then it's something worth talking about.

"I Couldn't Care More!"
-Jesus

God is with us. That is no answer for suffering. It is an answer to the sufferer.

God gives us no platitudes, no proverbs. He gives presence.

When Jesus spoke of suffering, He gave no easy answers. He told us simply that God is with us. He knows and notices the smallest things—a sparrow's death, a falling hair, a wilting lily.

Jesus gave no logical, philosophical explanation of how tragedies may strike or why. He only assured us that it was not His Father's will that anyone—not even the littlest of us—should perish.

Jesus gave no theological justification for all the evil and pain that surround us.

He gave us Himself. The clearest demonstration of how far God's suffering love will go.

When You Love

When you love others,
you love them as they are—
   not as you wish them to be,
   not as you hope to help them become,
   but as they are.
When you love others,
you love them because they are they—
   not loving in order to change them,
   not loving as a way of remaking them,
   but loving because you love.
When you love others,
you love them warts and all—
   not blinding yourself to their faults,
   not denying their imperfections,
   but loving in spite of. (God did.)
To love another
   is to reach out in hope
   for your love to awaken love
   in the heart of the other. (God does.)

Our Daily Bread

Fifteen thousand people will die of hunger—today. That's the size of my home city—fifteen thousand. Not suddenly wiped out, but slowly, finally expiring after the long wasting of starvation.

They need food. Not luxury amounts like those of us with expanded waistlines have in the West, but subsistent diets. Food to live.

Viewed in the light of world need, our household magazines dedicated to the worship of material things and luxury items are more obscene than the girlie magazines.

It is up to us who are taught by our Lord to pray for daily bread to break that bread in awareness that it was meant not just for me and mine but for all mankind.

Do we dare pray in His words, and then eat without acting to share?

Is Marriage Becoming Obsolete?

Marriage: Like flies on a windowpane. Those in want out, those out want in—1920.

Caution: Marriage may be hazardous to your health—1970.

This marriage license valid for ninety days. Renewable only upon consent of both parties, for a period of two years—1980?

Is marriage approaching obsolescence?

The Christian understands marriage as a covenant made under God and in the presence of fellow members of the Christian family. A covenant more solemn, more binding, more permanent than any legal contract.

God Himself has been called as witness to their act. God Himself has joined them together. What God has joined together, they will not let man put asunder.

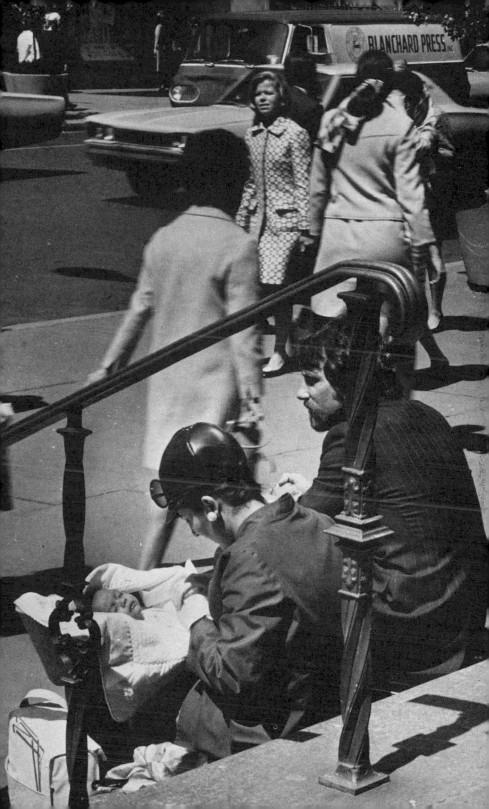

Creative Worry

Do you have a problem with worry?

Don't stop. That's been your problem. You quit too soon. Lay out your negative worries. Look at them honestly.

Then go on. To creative brooding. To creative worry.

You don't like the word? Then call it *imagineering,* meaning, "Let your imagination soar and then engineer it down to earth."

Or call it *visioneering.* Envision the best. Then claim it and attempt it for God.

You have a special weakness for worry? Strength can come from your weakness.

See visions. Dream dreams. Worry new work to be done. You may be on the edge of something great. Create!

Death Cannot Divide Us

Death will not divide us
from Him, our Lord.
Death is no solo venture.
We walk it with Him.
He walked it once alone,
that we need not.
He suffered death,
in Godforsaken sorrow,
yet never doubting
the morrow would break
with light eternal.
Now, death, the great divider,
is powerless before Him.
He steps through death
with us, as we awake
to life in full awareness.
To be absent from the body
is to be present with the Lord.

Hell: Heaven's Greatest Compliment

One of the greatest compliments you will ever receive is hell.

Hell, a compliment? Yes.

A compliment to your freedom. Your freedom to choose your destiny forever.

A compliment to the integrity God has given you. Your decisions matter. Ultimately.

A compliment to your personhood. If you become a true person before God, so you shall be through all eternity.

It's all up to you. You decide. You alone.

It's a Friendly Universe

Near the end of his life, the great English historian H. G. Wells was still searching for ultimate meaning.

If he could ask the timeless Egyptian sphinx one question from all the centuries it has observed, Wells said that question would be: "Is this universe hostile, is it neutral, or is it friendly?"

Headline it!

It's a friendly universe from the hand of a friendly Creator. From a God who is on your side against evil.

God is for you. God accepts you. God is love.

The Medicine of Laughter

Laughter is God's medicine. Spiritually, laughter is akin to praise. It is the natural response to joy. A good soul-stirring laugh is near to a prayer.

If God is love—then rejoice that all can be forgiven.

If God is joy—then celebrate Him.

Let your life come alive to His joyous presence. Let your thoughts feel the lilt of His laughter within you.

It's Your Choice

Life—from start to finish—is a matter of choices.

Which direction? Which decision? Which destiny? Which way shall you take?

Choices, no matter how small, do matter. Your day-to-day decisions have a way of determining your destiny.

The person you are becoming—situation by situation, decision by decision, choice by choice—is the person you will be forever.

Your central commitment may be to yourself. Or your central concern may be for others.

But if your central concern and commitment is to both God and man, as Jesus Christ's commitment was, then a whole new perspective on decision-making emerges. And what's more, a whole new strength to decide rightly becomes available.

It's your choice.